WALKS WITH MR. SMITH

WALKS WITH MR. SMITH

Damon Eddy

ISBN: 978-0-557-53881-2

To my incredible family that God has given me. My beautiful wife and the love of my life Julie, who I love more and more each day. My three special boys, Liam, Jace, and Brok, who I see and get excited for the impact they do and will make in this world. My little Hope, who was truly a gift from God.

CONTENTS

Preface vii

Chapter 1 Sound Familiar? 1

Chapter 2 Meeting Mr. Smith 3

Chapter 3 The Opportunity 11

Chapter 4 Be Thankful: Count Them One by One 17

Chapter 5 Seek Your Passion 23

Chapter 6 An Apple a Day 27

Chapter 7 Tenacity Got the Worm 33

Chapter 8 Attitude Gives Altitude 37

Chapter 9 Get Out of the Cave: The Gifts of Relationships 41

Chapter 10 The Lifelong Plan: Never Stop Learning 45

Chapter 11 Give Back: We Are the Hands 51

Chapter 12 The Final Walk 55

Chapter 13 Meeting Mrs. Smith 59

Mr. Smith's Life Lessons 69

Discussion Guide and Workbook 71

PREFACE

I first want to thank you for taking the time and putting forth the effort to read this book. Hopefully, the time will fly by, and the effort will be minimal. Better yet, I hope you won't want to put it down and read it all the way through, being moved and inspired to start or continue to live life to its fullest.

Have you ever wanted more out of life? Have you ever thought you could be doing more? Have you ever felt as though you were going backwards instead of forward? Have you ever thought you might not be reaching your full potential? Have you ever felt you weren't being a good spouse, parent, or friend? Have you ever thought that God put you on this Earth to do more than what you are currently doing or pursuing?

If you answered yes to any of these questions, this book will help if applied. Life can be frustrating. It can and is hard. There is no doubt in that. It can also be fulfilling and rewarding. It can be exciting and filled with adventure. You can have more out of life. You can be doing more. You can move forward each day. You can be moving toward your full potential. You can be a great spouse, parent, or friend and leave the level of being just good for others.

There is often a time in someone's life where they turn a corner. They say to themselves, "Enough is enough." They are tired of not doing. They always say, "I should do that, or I should do this." Eventually for some, the overwhelming guilt they always feel becomes too painful that the decision to change occurs. Sometimes, the change happens out of necessity and survival. Whatever the case may be, that turning point does come for a few. They leave no man's land, a world in which life is okay but not bad enough to really do anything about it. Many of us live in that land. We just stay where we are doing the same okay stuff every day. The life of passion and adventure seems left for others to play out on the big screen. Turning the corner or the thought of taking a new course seems impossible or does not ever cross the mind of many.

For you, it may be different. You are reading this. That in itself tells me you may be looking for change. You may want to turn that corner.

This story is about a man who turned that corner. Looking in, many from the outside would have thought he had it all. However, inside, he felt the opposite. He felt frustrated, guilty, overwhelmed, and unease every day, and he needed change. With his decision to change, a powerful gift was given. That gift was a relationship that changed Richard's life forever.

CHAPTER 1

SOUND FAMILIAR?

It had been a few months since the move. Richard was feeling a little let down as he was driving home from a hard day of dealing with impatient clients.

Is this what I worked so hard to achieve? I have a beautiful wife who loves me tremendously, four incredible children, a brand-new dream home, and a new car. What more could I need? Why do I feel this way? What is this uneasiness? Am I the only one who feels this way? Silly thought. I know I'm not.

Richard felt this way often. He was a hard worker, and he put tremendous pressure on himself. From the outside, no one would have known the turmoil he often felt inside. He felt he could and should be doing more, closing more deals, making more money, spending more time with his wife and kids, and exercising more. The pressure and frustration were getting to be too much. Something had to change. He felt as though he should be doing this and doing that. There were too many shoulds, but not enough action.

"I've had it! Enough is enough! I need some change. I don't know what, but I'm going to start tonight," Richard yelled as he crossed the railroad tracks close to his home.

The time had come for a change. He rolled down the window to feel the cool Colorado air. The windows were closed during the day because he was continually on his cell phone, dealing with things. He was always trying to hold things together. He looked in his rearview mirror, and he could see the sun starting to set behind the Rockies. The rays were shooting from behind the mountains, as if to highlight the large clouds above. It was a beautiful sight, one that Richard often missed. He lived in such a beautiful setting, but never seemed to have the time to enjoy or appreciate it. Even his drive home was scenic, but he often had the phone plastered to his ear. He didn't notice anything around him until he was pulling into his garage.

Tonight though, things needed to change. They would change. I've had enough.

CHAPTER 2
MEETING MR. SMITH

R ichard was anticipating his time alone. There are times in a person's life when he needs a change. A person becomes so frustrated and gets tired of always thinking about what he should be doing but is not. When that frustration reaches a certain level, change needs to happen. Richard had reached that level. No matter how small the change was, he was excited he had decided to take time to himself to walk and think. Before they moved here, Richard had told himself he'd do that once they moved. However, days, weeks, and months went by with no walks. Not anymore, however. He was done with the guilt.

Renée put their little girl to bed, and Richard was in charge of the boys. It always seemed to go a little smoother that way. Tristin, the oldest; Kaleb, the second-oldest; Ty; the youngest boy, and Sarah were all secure in their rooms for the night. Richard and Renée made it a habit every night to tuck each child in. After their teeth were brushed, their prayers were said, their nightlights were turned on, and their foreheads were kissed, they were secure. Tristin, who was now close to twelve, preferred just a rub on the head or fist bump. All were ready to sleep and recharge for the Saturday ahead.

They loved Richard. He was a good father. He had always told himself he would wake up his kids and put them to bed with love. For the most part, he had stuck to that routine. Richard was a giving and caring person. However, he realized he also needed to take care of himself. He could then better care for others.

Richard came downstairs, where Renée was running her bath.

"I'm going to go for my walk," he mentioned.

"What walk?" she said.

"Remember, I told you how I wanted to take walks around our neighborhood once we moved."

"I don't, but it sounds like a great idea. The loop is about a mile, so that will give you exercise and plenty of time." A beautiful paved road, outlined with trees, circled their neighborhood.

"It's something I want to do and truly be consistent with. We both talk about starting things, but find it hard to follow through." Richard made sure to be sensitive with his comments, as Renée had been talking about working out more.

"I know. It's hard with all the kids," she replied with a discouraged tone.

"That's why I think it's important we take time to do small things for ourselves, like you taking your bath." Richard noticed she was ready to get in.

He was sure she was tired and needed peace and quiet as much as he did. He had worked all day, and she had been with all four children. Richard knew that being a mom to four young children was one of the hardest jobs one could have.

***

Richard put on his sweatpants and a light sweatshirt. It was a brisk, stormy night, as it often was in September on the Colorado plains. This made for exciting nights with lightning illuminating the sky and thunder cracking through the air. As he stepped out, he felt the breeze hit his face. Richard looked toward the sky and noticed the moon in the east giving good light. Although not full, it lit the large, scattered storm clouds and showed a nice outline of the road. The walk seemed more private because no streetlights were on their road. Nobody was out in the neighborhood. There were less than two dozen beautiful homes that a large, circular street connected. All the home sites were on two acres of land or more. Aside from the people who lived there, the only other traffic was from curious individuals.

This was Richard's neighborhood. It was where he built his dream home and where he and Renée would raise their children and grow old together. He walked down his gravel driveway and toward the paved road. He felt an excitement move over his body, the kind one might feel when he knows something good is about to happen to him.

"Thank you, Lord, for giving me the discipline to start," Richard said.

He stepped onto the black pavement, and he began to remove the thoughts of the day from his mind and focus on the sound of the wind blowing through the cottonwoods. Richard looked up and admired the clouds painting the sky and the moon lighting the night. He walked at a slow pace. He wanted to make sure it was the opposite pace of his busy days. Trying to keep his clients, his wife, and four children happy kept him running. There would be no running this night. He'd just have time to think. He knew a better way was out there. This wasn't what he thought life would be. These walks were his start to try to find peace and that better way.

A few minutes into his walk, as he looked ahead, he noticed a neighbor walking toward the road. Richard hadn't been in the neighborhood long. He had only met the neighbors to the immediate sides of his house. He had a tendency to stay to himself. Richard slowed down. He wanted to see what this man's plan was.

If he were just going to get his mail, then perfect.

At their current paces, the men would inevitably meet up with one another soon.

This is supposed to be my time alone. I don't want to meet someone, much less have to take my walk with a stranger. I meet enough people throughout the day.

The man glanced toward Richard. At that point, it was too late for Richard to turn around without it seeming obvious.

"Good evening," the man said. He was a few feet from stepping onto the pavement and only fifteen feet from Richard.

Richard replied unenthusiastically, thinking it might discourage anymore conversation. "Good evening to you as well."

"It's a beautiful night for a stroll. Would you mind if I join you?" the man asked.

It simply wasn't right to say no to a neighbor. Richard was a considerate man, and he never liked to hurt anyone's feelings, much less come across as a jerk.

"Sure. That would be great. It can get a little scary out here at night with the foxes and coyotes," Richard joked.

"I can't remember the last time I heard of a fox attacking someone in our area, but there's strength in numbers," the man replied with a warm smile.

Richard noticed the man had a large, solid build. The man was not overweight, but just well built. To his best guess, he was just as tall as Richard, who stood around six foot four. He wore a wool hat on his head, and he dressed warmer than what the night called for. Richard would have put the man's age in his seventies.

"My name is Mr. Smith. May I have the pleasure of your name, sir?" He spoke in an eloquent, sophisticated tone. He shook Richard's hand firmly while clutching his shoulder with his left hand. Richard noticed the enormous size of the man's hands.

"Richard. Richard Thims." Mr. Smith's introduction almost intimidated him.

"New to the neighborhood, are you? I noticed the lights at your home in the evening on a consistent basis. Beautiful home you have."

"Thank you. We moved about three weeks ago. I always dreamed about building my dream home, so we are pretty excited."

"Dreams are powerful. Too many do not dream. They dream when they are children, but then somehow stop when they grow older. The days take their dreams, goals, and ambitions until they faintly exist or don't exist at all. The truly successful take from the day, using it as an ally and helping them reach their goals and passions. You might say they keep the spark alive."

Richard admired what he just heard. He listened to some personal development speakers and read a few books. But he had never actually heard someone speak with so much confidence and passion about dreaming, ambition, and goals unless at a seminar in which the individual was being paid to do so.

"Well said. I couldn't agree more. It's hard though to keep the passion and not get caught up in the business of the day. That's something I'm struggling with." Richard realized how at ease and oddly comfortable he felt while speaking to a man he had just met.

"Is that the reason for your walk tonight?" Mr. Smith asked as if he knew.

"Yes, it is. I figured I'd take time to slow down and reflect on the past week. I'd use the moments alone to myself to try to find answers on how I could improve and become a better person."

Richard realized he and Mr. Smith had been strolling at a slow pace down the road. Richard looked back at Mr. Smith's home and noticed only one light on in one of the bay windows. Driving by the home in the day, he always admired the incredibly manicured lawn and landscaped mounds. He never saw a hint of one weed, something that was hard to do where they lived. He never saw anyone in the yard, however. He sometimes found it strange.

Looking closer, Richard noticed a silhouette of a person standing in the window. The light from what must have been a lamp, along with the faint curtain, gave an outline of a woman. Incredibly still, there was no movement, as if she were a statue.

Mr. Smith startled Richard. "What a great idea these walks."

"Yes, it will be good. Is that the missus in the window?" Richard continued to look back at the distant silhouette.

"Why, yes. The love of my life. We've been married forty-six years. God couldn't have given me a better companion." Mr. Smith smiled softly as they continued their walk.

"Any children?"

"We have four. Three incredibly blessed boys and a beautiful daughter. They've given us ten wonderful grandchildren to play with."

Intrigued with the similarity to his family, Richard started to reply, but Mr. Smith answered first. "Sound familiar?"

"Yes, it sure does."

"I can see why you need these walks. Three boys and a little girl is a big job."

"Oh, have you met my wife and kids before?" Richard was somewhat confused as to how Mr. Smith knew about his children. He had never seen Mr. Smith in the day. Renée had never mentioned ever meeting any other neighbors.

"Us old folks know more than you think. Beautiful night, isn't it?" Mr. Smith replied as they continued their walk.

"It really couldn't be any nicer."

How does Mr. Smith seem to know about my kids? Maybe just a coincidence? Maybe he saw them playing in the yard?

Richard couldn't believe how easy it was to speak to Mr. Smith. Richard was good with people, but was often the quiet one and careful always to not say too much. He more or less liked to listen. He also didn't want to reveal so much of himself. It made him less vulnerable. But this was different. He felt safe. It was if he were talking to an old friend he hadn't seen. There was catching up to do. On that walk, Richard had managed to tell Mr. Smith what seemed like his whole life story. It was something he rarely, if at all, had done with anyone.

As they came around the circle close to Richard's home, Mr. Smith said, "Richard, I have greatly enjoyed our walk. You remind me so much of myself when I was your age."

"I have enjoyed it as well."

"I'm an older man now, but, listening to you speak, I can see and hear a passionate young man who is looking to do better. Who wants to improve. That is a great quality. I have lived a long life and raised four incredibly happy and healthy children. I am blessed with wonderful grandchildren. I have traveled the world, and I have had incredible people impact my life. I have been fortunate to do the same for many."

Richard listened and realized that Mr. Smith might just be the mentor that was so important in a man's life. All the popular books always stressed relationships and taking advantage of opportunities when they were presented. Mr. Smith seemed like that gift, that opportunity. Although Richard was spilling his life information the whole time, it seemed healing. It felt good. He had wanted to say things, but, up until that point, he wasn't comfortable telling. This wasn't the case, however, with Mr. Smith. He felt safe.

"I can see why you have. You are easy to talk to, and you have an inviting presence," Richard complimented.

"Thank you. You are kind. I have enjoyed our walk together. I would love for us to continue our conversation with other walks. It would be beneficial for both of us to discuss what many call the ever-challenging game of life."

I should be the one asking Mr. Smith. What a great opportunity.

"I would love to, if you would. I was planning to take these walks once a week. Friday nights seemed like a good evening. Once I put the kids to bed, between nine and ten. What works for you?"

"Richard, don't worry about my schedule. At my age, you don't have too many pressing matters filling your time. How about this? You go in and spend time with your wife. It's getting late. We will agree to Friday evening and meet up just like we did. When you are ready, just start walking. I will meet you."

"Should we set an exact time? Do you want me to call you?" Richard wanted to give Mr. Smith some kind of notice.

"No need. Just start your walk when you are ready. I will be there." Mr. Smith stopped and shook Richard's hand while extending his free arm over Richard's shoulders, again squeezing firmly. He then looked Richard in the eyes. "See you Friday." He continued down the road.

"See you then." Richard was still confused as to how Mr. Smith would know when he was coming.

Mr. Smith seemed not worried, however, so Richard did not press. From the end of his driveway, Richard stood and watched Mr. Smith continue down the moonlit street toward his home. For an elder gentleman, Mr. Smith walked extremely upright with a very smooth gait.

He doesn't move like most older men.

Mr. Smith seemed to move with little effort. Richard stood and just listened. He took in the sounds of the night before he went back into the house. He shut his eyes and felt the light breeze of the night. He listened to the bush crickets filling the night, along with the chorus frogs that were a popular pet for his boys in the day. The light rustling of the leaves from the cottonwoods gave a soothing sound. He heard the distant dog barks that the activities around were triggering. Raccoons, coyotes, skunks, and unusually bold foxes often frustrated his dogs on occasion. They would bark from their kennels. Where they lived, if one had dogs outside at night, it was wise to put them in a kennel for their protection. The coyote packs would often lure dogs away from their homes and sometimes kill or, at the very least, keep the local veterinarians busy.

Richard took in deep breaths and felt peace, something he wasn't feeling enough of in his life.

What a great night. What great conversation.

Along with that peace, he felt energized and renewed. He opened his eyes and looked down the road to where he last saw Mr. Smith. He was excited for their next meeting. He would sleep well that night.

CHAPTER 3
THE OPPORTUNITY

R ichard didn't sleep well that night, much less any of the other nights that week. He was busy. The demands of life took over. Work seemed to take up most of his time. Reflecting back, Richard felt disappointed for the job he had done, better yet, not done as a husband and father. He seemed to be dealing with clients starting early in the morning until late at night. When interacting with Renée or the kids, that was really all it was, interacting. His mind was often somewhere else, thinking of what needed to be done, what call he needed to make, and what lead he needed to follow up with. He forgot the reason he was doing what he did was right in front of him, his beautiful wife and kids.

"What a week," Richard said to Renée as they cleaned up from their kids pre-bedtime snack.

Pre-bedtime snacks were a ritual. They usually consisted of a bowl of cereal, something the kids could actually make.

"Yeah, you seemed pretty busy. We didn't get to see you that much this week."

Richard could sense the twinge of frustration. In many instances, he might get mad as he wouldn't think Renée was being supportive. However, he understood why she'd be bothered.

"I know. I feel bad. This isn't the way it should be. I haven't put you and the kids first. It isn't right to put my job ahead of my family."

"We're extremely blessed. We have a wonderful home and a good income. I'm extremely proud of you. You're a hard worker, and I appreciate that about you. You're providing. Remember, however, that we need your love. I'm not saying this out of anger, but out of love. I need you. The kids need you. Not the money or things, but you."

Richard knew she was right. He felt terrible. He could feel the tears begin to well up. He felt the emptiness inside.

"You're so right. I haven't been giving time to you and the kids. I've been working to give you and the kids a nice home and things, but how crazy of me not to give you what you want most, a husband and father to your children. The frustrating thing is I know this, but I still get caught up."

Seeing the pain and sincere heartache Richard was feeling, Renée stopped Richard from his dishwashing. She grabbed him tightly around his waist and looked into his eyes.

"I love you. We love you. You're the most important person on this earth to the children and me. We don't need things. We need you. That's the best gift all of us could ever ask for."

Richard was an extremely sensitive man. Crying wasn't a problem for him. He could see the honesty in Renée's voice. A tear rolled down the side of his cheek. Renée kissed it, and they embraced. It felt good.

***

The kids were asleep, and the kitchen was cleaned. Renée took her place in the chair in the great room, ready to relax in peace after a long day with the kids. She was tired and had every reason to be. Richard sat next to her on the couch. It was quiet, something often rare in a house full of rambunctious boys and a demanding little girl.

"You better hit the trail, mister. Don't want to keep our neighbor waiting," Renée said jokingly.

"I know. I'd better get out there. It's getting late." Richard got up from his very comfortable position.

"What time were you supposed to meet him?"

"He said he'd just know. It was almost as if he could see me coming somehow. I thought it strange. Maybe he can see up the street from his house. Not sure."

"Well, it's nine o'clock. My show is on, so have fun on your walk. I'm going to sit here and veg out." Renée grabbed the remote.

Richard put on his sweatshirt, along with a parka vest. The nights were beginning to cool down. People had mentioned that it was going to be an early winter that year. Some of Richard's newly landscaped trees were giving those indications as well. A few of his recently planted cottonwoods were turning. His hackberries were already losing their leaves.

After stepping outside, the dogs, who would have loved nothing more than to accompany Richard on his walk, greeted him. They had a tendency, however, to get distracted and set their own course. Richard didn't feel like having to deal with that, so he gave them a dog biscuit and put them in their kennel for the night. Getting the dog biscuit was a very close second to a preferred walk for them. They were happy with their second choice.

It was a very light night. The moon looked full. Very little clouds were in the sky. Richard's eyes were already beginning to adjust, and he could clearly see his surroundings. As he stepped onto the asphalt, he could hear the many barks of the distant dogs. They were restless that night. Richard assumed that, because they could see better, they could see more things moving. He wasn't an expert, however, on night animal activity.

As he walked, he could hear the wind rustling through the large, old cottonwoods that surrounded his street. It was cool. He was glad he decided to wear his vest. He was a little anxious about meeting Mr. Smith again. A little of that anxiousness was not knowing if he would be seeing him that night. It was late.

Just then, Richard could see him. Mr. Smith was coming up his driveway in the exact place that he originally saw him their previous meeting. It was much lighter this night, so Richard would be able to see his walking partner much clearer than their previous walk.

"Mr. Smith, how are you this evening?" Richard spoke in a louder tone as they were still about twenty feet from each other.

"Great, Richard! I feel great. How is my walking partner this evening?" Speaking with enthusiasm, Mr. Smith's voice seemed powerful yet soothing to Richard.

"I am good as well."

"I said great. Let's see if we can get you from good to great before the night is through," Mr. Smith said jokingly.

"Sounds perfect, Mr. Smith."

"Good," Mr. Smith replied with a warm smile as he grabbed Richard with his arm.

Richard usually liked to keep more distance between people unless it was Renée or the kids. However, it felt okay with Mr. Smith.

Because it was a bright night, Richard was able to study his new friend better than their previous meeting. He was quickly drawn to Mr. Smith's large eyes which seem to look into Richard's soul. Still to dark to tell the color, the whites of Mr. Smith's eyes indicated that he had great vitality and energy for a man his age. They looked strangely familiar to Richard. Strong cheekbones framed his companion's mouth which arched into the warmest smile Richard had ever seen from a man. It was obvious that the man standing in front of him was special.

"How was your week?" Mr. Smith put his hand on Richard's shoulder as they continued down the street.

"I got caught up again. Renée actually spoke with me tonight about how she and the kids missed me. She was supportive and appreciated what I was doing, but made it clear that the best gift they could have was me. More of my time."

"Understood. You have so much to offer, Richard, as a husband and father. Our life is so much about relationships. Those relationships with the ones closest to us can either be a tremendous source of joy and energy, or they can be our greatest source of pain, guilt, and frustration in our lives."

"I understand. It seems so hard to be able to give everyone what they seem to need."

"The key word you just said is seem, which may be a little bit of the problem. In relationships, we need not guess at what the other person may need. We need to find out. In your business, do you kinda try to give your client what he needs?"

"No, I find out his needs and then make every attempt to meet them." Richard knew where Mr. Smith was going.

"Why then would you not find out the needs of the people you most love in this world and work incredibly to satisfy those needs? Seems to make sense, does it not?" Mr. Smith kept a steady pace as they walked.

"You're right. It makes complete sense. Strange how most people, including myself, don't truly find out the needs of the people closest to them. It's as though we take them for granted."

Mr. Smith stopped walking and faced Richard. "There are many things that make complete sense. The problem is that most people choose not to do them. A few people, however, do the things that make sense, and they live much more fulfilling lives. They live with a passion and sense of purpose. They have the incredible relationships. They give and not worry about receiving. So many little things are done differently. Those little things, however, make all the difference."

Richard stood listening, as if in a trance, and focused on every word that was said.

"Richard, I had the privilege to have someone teach me some very valuable life lessons when I was your age. An incredible mentor came into my life. It made all the difference to me. I was very much like you. I was successful in my career, and I had a beautiful family. But inside, I was confused, not satisfied, and felt very little peace. Once that mentor taught me the lessons, I was able to head a new direction in my life, a direction that leads to more success not only in the workplace but, most importantly, at home and with others. It led me on a life journey where I have been privileged to watch not only my wife and children find incredible peace, happiness, and success in their lives, but millions of others as well."

Who is this man? What profession would be able to impact as many as Mr. Smith has?

Richard responded, "Mr. Smith, what did you do? What was your occupation?"

"Richard, I was fortunate to help others."

"So you were a speaker? Teacher? Author?"

"I was many things, and I still have a little energy left in me to help one more." Mr. Smith seemed to not really answer Richard's question.

Richard was smart. With his experience dealing with people on a daily basis, he knew when someone was not or did not feel comfortable giving out more information about himself. This he felt with Mr. Smith.

"Are you saying you'd give me the honor of being your student?" Richard smiled as they continued their slow pace around the last turn on their walk, nearing Richard's home.

"If you'd give me the opportunity, this old man may have just enough energy for his last student."

"I don't know about last student. You look like you're in pretty good shape. Heck, are you thinking it will take that long to fix me?"

They both laughed. They had reached Richard's home. Mr. Smith lived two houses down. Richard enjoyed the time so much that he offered to continue the walk to Mr. Smith's place. "Want me to continue down to your house, Mr. Smith?"

"Oh, no. You have a lovely wife inside, who I'm sure wants to visit with her man. I'll see you next Friday for our first lesson."

"Should I bring a pen and pad?" Richard asked jokingly.

"Not unless you can write and walk in the dark all at the same time."

"Understood. Thank you, sir."

"No, thank you, Richard. I look forward to our time together."

Mr. Smith turned and continued down the road. Richard stopped halfway up his driveway and watched Mr. Smith until he seemed to fade in the night.

CHAPTER 4
BE THANKFUL: COUNT THEM ONE BY ONE

A storm was coming in that night. Richard stepped out onto his covered deck and looked at the large storm clouds rolling in from the north. The wind was blowing hard, but not too cold. It was still September, so nothing like what the wind would be three months from then. Closing his eyes, Richard felt the cool breeze on his cheeks. All he could hear were the leaves stirring and the rush of the wind. He felt a sense of calm and quietness that was absent to him most of the week. He inhaled deeply, as if to take in the energy the night was offering.

After a few moments, Richard opened his eyes. He felt renewed and energized for his time with Mr. Smith. Although windy and ominous, Richard knew the rain wouldn't start for another hour or so. The clouds seemed to not be in a hurry. An hour would be perfect for his walk with Mr. Smith. He had been looking forward to their time together all week. Although Richard had a better week than the previous, he still felt lost.

Realizing it was a little colder than expected, Richard stepped back in the house for another layer of clothes. Renée had just sat down from her day, which dealt with cooking meals for three hungry boys and a little girl who seemed to have just as big of an appetite as her brothers, not to mention all the in-between snacks dirtying what was just cleaned. The sibling arguments, dirty diapers, homework time ... You name it.

It was work. Richard knew his job was easier in many ways than what Renée dealt with on a daily basis. He appreciated her and hoped she knew it. He sometimes felt she might not, but wanted to do better. He wanted to let her know.

"You heading out for your walk?"

"Yes, it's colder tonight so I'm just going to get a jacket. Do you need anything?"

"No, I'm good."

Richard walked over to Renée and sat down next to her. "Are you sure? Do you want me to get you some water? Tea? Hot chocolate?"

"You're sweet. I'm fine. Thank you. Do you need anything? You worked hard this week."

"You worked harder. You do a great job with the kids. My job is easier." Richard wanted Renée to feel the appreciation that she deserved.

"I don't know if I worked harder. I'll, however, agree that your job is easier though."

Both laughed. Richard put his hand on her thigh and lightly squeezed it.

"You're right. So, if you're okay, I'm going to meet Mr. Smith."

"Sounds good. He seems like an interesting man. I'm glad you found a walking partner."

Richard got up. "Me, too."

Richard weaved his way through the pile of shoes, toys, bikes, and various other objects the kids seemed to collect and place just outside the garage door. He made his way to the street. He stepped onto the road, stopped for a moment, and shut his eyes, as he always seemed to do when wanting to relax. It was his way of shutting out the worries of the day and preparing for the time ahead. He heard nothing but the quietness of the night. It was nice, and it was peace. It was still. It was opposite of what his days were. He opened his eyes and began toward Mr. Smith's home. He walked down the moonlit road and looked at the trees swaying gently back and forth with the wind. His glance moved down the road. He then saw Mr. Smith walking up his driveway, heading toward the road. Richard fixed his eyes on the distant friend and studied as much as he could, the smooth walk and the large build.

Approaching closer, Richard wanted to be the first to greet. "Good evening, sir," he spoke in a loud tone, knowing some distance was still between them.

"Good evening to you as well, my walking partner," Mr. Smith responded in what Richard had come to know as an amazingly powerful voice that seemed to carry effortlessly.

Instead of the handshake this time, Mr. Smith immediately put his arm around Richard's shoulders and gave him a squeeze. Again, not being the touchy-feely type, this felt okay. Mr. Smith felt like family to him. He felt like a father excited to catch up with his son who had come back from college, war, or a distant trip. Heck, Richard felt as if he'd been in a war some weeks.

Richard looked into Mr. Smith's vibrant eyes. "How have you been this past week?"

"Could not have been better. I'm extremely blessed."

"You seem happy and excited." Richard studied Mr. Smith's face, which seemed to radiate energy. It gave him the appearance of being thirty years younger.

"The fact I've been given another day to meet with you is enough to make me happy," replied Mr. Smith.

"You're too kind." Richard thought to himself that, before him, was a man twice his age, yet filled with more enthusiasm than himself or most men he knew.

Richard glanced back to Mr. Smith's home and saw the light by the bay window, along with the very still silhouette of Mrs. Smith.

She must have been standing.

Focused on the window as if entranced, Mr. Smith startled Richard. "I'm kind because I'm happy. I'm happy because I'm blessed. I'm blessed because I'm aware."

"Aware of what?" Richard focused off Mr. Smith's home and back on the road ahead.

"My blessings."

"Your blessings? Your things?" Richard asked.

"Well, you could say things, but I like to be more specific. You know, this is actually our first lesson."

"I was wondering how you were going to bring it up."

"Richard, I have a knack for teaching and a way of getting my points across." Mr. Smith laughed slightly. It was more at himself than anything else.

"I can tell you wouldn't have any trouble getting points across to others. I remember a TV ad when I was younger about Dean Witter. 'When Dean Witter speaks, people listen.' When Mr. Smith talks, everyone listens." Richard, still somewhat new to the relationship, thought he was being funny, but realized it was a lame joke. He laughed and humbly responded, "That wasn't too funny."

"The fact you admit it wasn't that funny makes up for it."

"Thanks. So what is our first lesson?" Richard was anxious to start learning. He knew Mr. Smith had a wealth of information. He might be the key to stop some of the turmoil and uneasiness that he so often felt. The student was ready; the teacher was there.

"Count your blessings. Be thankful daily. The Bible teaches us to be overflowing with thankfulness. Let me ask you a question, Richard. How thankful are you daily?"

"Now that you mention it, I don't think I am. It seems I'm often complaining more than anything. I'm good at not complaining to others because that's a trait I don't like. However, inside, I'm complaining to myself."

Mr. Smith replied as if he made a discovery, although he was too smart for Richard's answer to be a surprise. "Ah, you see, my friend, that is something that needs to change. I would suggest that, when your wife has gone to sleep tonight and everyone is taken care of, you find a nice comfortable spot and make a list. This list needs to consist of everything you are thankful for. I would suggest you start with yourself."

"What do you mean?" Richard wanted to make sure he fully understood what Mr. Smith was asking.

"Are you healthy?"

"Why, yes."

"Good. That's a start. Not to sound too simplistic, but how much would you give for your right arm? How about both arms?"

"Well, if you ask it like that, it would be hard to put a price on them. They are incredibly valuable to me."

"What about the legs you are walking on? What about your mind that God has given you? Your two eyes allow you to see the beauty around you. In Proverbs 20:12, it is pointed out that we should be grateful for our eyes and ears. You see, Richard, one doesn't have to look any further than himself to find things to be thankful for. The day in itself is a gift. Try not living one."

They both laughed at Mr. Smith's remark. It was true what he was saying, but Richard had never taken the time to be thankful for the simple things. He began to think about all the blessings he did have: his wife, his children, his health, his job, his home, and his abilities.

"People always have a tendency to focus on what they do not have. Now, I am not saying it is wrong to be ambitious, but, if you want happiness in your life, you first must be thankful for what you have been given. Only from the place of true thankfulness can one then proceed to the life God would want for him. Pursuing more with an unthankful heart only leads to unrest, frustration, and unhappiness. Pursuing a vision or goal with thankfulness will create passion, courage, hope, and a sense of excitement and fulfillment in one's life."

While Mr. Smith spoke, Richard focused on all he had been given. He focused on his incredibly loving wife, his four healthy children, the wonderful home in which they lived, and the time with Mr. Smith. A feeling of excitement passed through him, just as Mr. Smith said. It was the excitement of what he had and what the future would hold.

"You're right. I feel better already." Richard wanted to let Mr. Smith know he was understanding what he was saying.

"Richard, you have so much to be grateful for. If you do not take the time to appreciate what you have been given, what then is the use of it being given to you in the first place?"

"Amazing. It seems so simple, but hard to do." Richard was frustrated with himself for missing such a simple concept every day.

Mr. Smith turned slightly toward Richard. He looked into his eyes as if to get his point across more. "It isn't as hard as you think. Every morning, count your blessings. If it means getting up ten minutes earlier, than do it. If it means taking two minutes sitting on the side of your bed before your feet hit the ground, do it. Don't wait another day. You will be amazed with the immediate impact it will have on your day and your life."

"I'm sure. I feel it now."

Arriving at the end of Richard's driveway, Mr. Smith looked at Richard's home. "What a beautiful gift your home is. Now go in there, grab a pen and paper, find a comfortable spot, and start to write down everything you're thankful for. This will help you in your mornings and lead us into our next lesson."

"Our next lesson. Any hints?" Richard hoped for a clue.

"No hints. I don't want you to figure it out and skip a week."

"You don't have to worry about that."

"Good. I'm enjoying our time together. Besides, this old man needs a young friend in his life."

Mr. Smith continued down the road. Richard slowly nodded in agreement.

Mr. Smith doesn't need a friend, but I need a friend like Mr. Smith.

Richard watched Mr. Smith fading into the night and thought deeply as to what was said. He was excited to begin his list.

CHAPTER 5
SEEK YOUR PASSION

R ichard had a much better week. He felt that much of it had to do with starting his days correctly. He had been good that week with being thankful each morning. It was sometimes done on the edge of his bed. Other times, it was in the shower. It was getting done, and he felt good because of it. The more grateful he became, the less unhappiness he felt. The two feelings seemed unable to coexist with one another.

Stepping onto the street that night, he felt excited again for his next lesson. Richard thought to himself how much the first lesson had helped him and only felt that it would get better from there. He was right.

***

"Do you have a vision?" Mr. Smith asked Richard.

"You mean goals?"

"That's a part of it. One has to proceed the other, however. You must first have a vision before you set correct goals. You have to know which harbor you are sailing for and which destination you are desiring. At that point, you can then chart your course, set your sail, and progress toward that destination daily."

Richard walked beside Mr. Smith. "That makes sense. I once heard that you have to think with the end in mind."

"Correct. You have to see yourself clearly reaching that destination. The clearer, the better. For example, let's say you want to take a romantic European vacation with your wife. The first thing you should do is develop a vivid image in your mind of the trip itself. Shut your eyes, and picture the scenery as the two of you hold hands and look out onto the French countryside as you ride the train. Maybe it is walking beside a lake in the Swiss Alps, just taking in the smell of the crisp air flowing up from the water. How about floating the canals in Venice as she lies in your arms and looks up at the incredible architecture? How about the two of you having dinner in a small, dimly lit café in Paris while sipping wine, looking into each other's eyes, and having incredible conversation as if the two of you only existed at that point in time?"

As they walked, Richard listened in amazement at the ideas that seemed to flow effortlessly out of Mr. Smith's mouth.

Who is this man? What a gift he is to me!

"Whatever vision you have, you must first create the outcome in your mind. The smell, the sounds, and the scenery have to be clear. You must feel the sensation and emotion in your body as if they have already happened. At that point, they can be written down on paper as goals, followed by the specific action steps needed to achieve those goals. If not a continual goal, a deadline is crucial as well."

Mr. Smith always looked at Richard. Very little did his eyes face the direction of their walk. It was as if Mr. Smith was just as mesmerized with Richard as Richard was with him. Maybe Mr. Smith saw in Richard much of himself when he was younger. Whatever it was, an incredible friendship was building.

Mr. Smith wanted his point to sink in. He remained quiet and gave Richard time.

After a minute, Richard responded, "So you have to write them down?"

"Of course. Consider it the first step of discipline needed for them to be achieved. If you can't take the first step of writing them down, more than likely, you will not be disciplined enough to take the proper actions for your dreams to be achieved. There's something magical and powerful when a man puts his dreams in life to pen to paper. It is as if he is letting the world know he is serious. The dreaming not only happens at night, but in the day. A man who dreams with his eyes wide open is a powerful man."

Richard nodded in agreement, as if he knew the answer to his previous question and to all that Mr. Smith said.

Mr. Smith stopped and faced Richard. "Richard, very few people actually set their course in life. They smother the vision that God had placed in their heart until it no longer exists. They live without passion. They settle, and they doubt. Is that how you want to live? Is that how you want your children to live?"

Richard felt a mix of frustration for his lack of vision and excitement from the power in the lesson he was hearing. "I don't want to live without passion. Of course, I want my children to go after their dreams."

"Then you have to go after yours." Mr. Smith placed both hands on Richard's shoulders. "You must set the example for them. They will do as you do. If you want a better marriage, then show them how to have one by living one. If you want them to be successful in the workplace, then show them what that means and looks like. If you want them to give back to society, then you must give back. Be the man you want them to be."

Richard dropped his head and stared at the dark pavement below, as if ashamed for the example he had been lately. Mr. Smith noticed the guilt his partner was feeling. He placed one of his hands on Richard and gave him a pat of encouragement.

"Richard, you have accomplished much. Don't feel that you haven't. However, this uneasiness you are feeling needs to be used to spur you to greater things. I see tremendous potential in you. I know you have dreams inside of you that are waiting to be realized. You have talents that need to be used and gifts that need to be opened. Don't leave them at your deathbed unused. Live a life without regrets. Understood?"

Richard took his glance upward toward the clear Colorado sky. He responded with just two simple words, "I do." The words from Mr. Smith seemed to hit him like a cold bucket of water to the face. It was an awakening.

"Richard, I know you have dreams you want to see realized. Those dreams create the vision. Take time this week to seek that vision for your life. From there, write your goals and the actions needed to be taken that coincide with the vision for you life with deadlines if appropriate. From there, you need to look at those goals daily. Keep your mind focused on them."

"I will."

"Great. And one last lesson."

Richard laughed slightly, as his mood was being lifted. "A bonus? Extra credit?"

"You could say." Mr. Smith waited a few seconds and said quietly, as if to make Richard focus more, "Take action. A firefly only lights up when it is flying, not sitting on a branch waiting. We light up when we are acting upon the vision and goals we set for our lives. Very few take action. Most wait. Do not wait. Always take action in the things you set out to do. That's your bonus. Now go do."

Mr. Smith squeezed Richard, as he often did. Then he proceeded down the road. The only words Richard could think of to say, he gave to Mr. Smith faintly. "Thank you."

It was a powerful night. Before going into his home, Richard walked to the back of his house and sat on the deck. He looked out into the dark night. As always, he could hear the distant barking of dogs, the rustling of the leaves, and the occasional yips of the coyotes causing trouble. He remembered the words Mr. Smith had spoken to him. Richard felt a warm sensation come over him. He began to think of what could be. He felt a great sense of hope for his future and the power it was giving. The vision and dreams began to enter Richard's mind. It was as if they were asleep in a long hibernation, but were slowly awakening and ready for their orders.

CHAPTER 6

AN APPLE A DAY

R ichard pulled onto his street on what was an incredibly warm Thursday afternoon in October. The sun was out, as it most often was, but, along with the sun, was a temperature in the mid-sixties. Richard was fortunate that he was able to set his own schedule. He was excited to come home and surprise Renée with a small bouquet of flowers he had picked up at the local florist.

While driving down his street, Richard focused his eyes on Mr. Smith's home, as he always did. Richard never saw Mr. Smith during the day. He was never in the yard. He was never driving in and out for errands. There was nothing.

The yard was immaculate. Beautiful pines were set on landscaped mounds. Several mounds held large boulders with small water features that trickled down to little ponds that were surrounded with small willows. If Richard were to guess, there were close to fifty trees on Mr. Smith's property, which was not normal for the plains of Colorado. The yard was the envy of the whole neighborhood. There wasn't a weed to be found.

But who maintained it?

Richard was again confused because he never saw anyone outside.

No Mrs. Smith. No gardener. No landscaper. I have some time. Maybe I'll stop by. It would be nice to see Mr. Smith in the day.

Richard had only seen Mr. Smith during their Friday night walks. Pulling into Mr. Smith's driveway, Richard felt nervous. It was as if he were breaking the rules. He felt as though he was intruding. He knew of the mutual admiration the two men felt, but never received an invite from Mr. Smith to stop by and visit during the day.

Stopping in front of Mr. Smith's home, he noticed all the window shades were pulled shut. As he slowly walked toward the front door, Richard was again amazed at the impeccable outside. The long, winding walkway led to the beautiful, solid mahogany door without one sign of the ever-present Colorado dust.

Standing in front of the large door, Richard again felt uneasy. He paused for a moment and thought if he should even knock.

How silly.

There was such a strong, comfortable feeling during the walks with Mr. Smith. Richard felt incredibly at ease during the nights. It was almost as if the daylight was going to reveal something previously unknown about his friend that Richard maybe was not up to deal with at the moment. Whatever it was, he felt the worry deep within himself.

Richard stood in front of the door and quietly listened to notice if he could hear any sign of the Smiths being home. Although he never saw them leave, he also never saw any sign of them being there as well. The only hints of life were when Mr. Smith walked out to meet Richard and Mrs. Smith's silhouette watching through the front window. Other than that, there was nothing.

As Richard raised his hand in hesitation to ring the doorbell, the loud ringing of his phone startled. He grabbed it quickly to not let his presence possibly known to the Smiths. Richard answered quietly. It was the school. One of his boys was sick and needed to be picked up. As Richard walked back to his car, he felt an odd sense of relief that he was called away from his possible day visit with Mr. Smith.

As he drove away, he looked back in his rearview mirror and noticed one of the front window curtains slightly open and then shut.

Someone is home.

Goose bumps flooded Richard's body. All he could think about the rest of the afternoon was that window and the Smiths. He greatly anticipated their next meeting.

***

The wind blew hard and stirred the brittle leaves as the last few were hanging on to the large branches of the cottonwoods. More found their home on the ground, blowing this way or that. Richard took in the sound and energy of the night and anticipated his next lesson. Looking down the road, he saw Mr. Smith walking down his driveway, the same as he had the previous Friday nights. Richard's eyes fixated on Mr. Smith's image in the distance with his ever-present fedora perched on his head. He noticed the large silhouette, the smooth, gliding walk, and the mysterious presence of a man he had only known a short time. Richard felt, along with his excitement, a sense of calming peace. It was much different from the feeling he'd had a few days earlier while stopping to visit Mr. Smith during the day. Richard then thought about the window.

Was that Mr. Smith behind the curtain? Mrs. Smith? Should I let Mr. Smith know I dropped by? Surely he would know.

"My friend, how are you tonight?" Mr. Smith stepped onto the road.

Richard, as always, was amazed at how such a powerful voice as Mr. Smith's could be as soothing as it was.

"Great. I couldn't be better."

Mr. Smith smiled. "Well, we will see if we can increase a little tonight."

The two men arrived next to one another. This time, Richard was the first to wrap his right arm around the shoulders of Mr. Smith and give a strong squeeze. Richard felt the large sturdiness of the man twice his age, or at least he assumed Mr. Smith was around that old. It was hard for Richard to tell. His energy, both physically and mentally, was that of a much younger man, but his longer, silver hair, deeply wrinkled face, and large, weathered hands told otherwise.

After the usual small talk, they dug right in to the next lesson.

"Richard, we last talked about finding your vision, setting goals, and taking action. What progress have you made?"

"To be honest, it has been amazing. I took time this past week and wrote down specific goals for each area of my life. It was exciting and gave me incredible energy."

"Great. You took action. You have now done more than what 97 percent of people never do. You have created a plan. You have drawn yourself a map to reach great destinations. Congratulations!"

"It does feel good. Now I need to just follow through. It's hard, as I'm sure you know, to find energy with all of the other responsibilities."

"Understood," Mr. Smith responded. "Energy is a precious commodity. If we don't have it, it's hard to get the things done that need to be. We need to have the fuel in our system if we want to go anywhere."

"I could use more fuel. Some high-octane stuff would be nice." Richard laughed.

Mr. Smith smiled. "Richard, you are segueing perfectly into our next lesson, living a healthy life."

"You mean exercise?"

"Exercise is a part of it. Let me ask you a question. It looks as though you do or have exercised in the past. Am I correct?"

"You are. I used to, but, with the kids and work, it is something I have been putting off. To be honest, I feel guilty every day that I don't. It used to be such an important part of my life. I just got busy."

"I understand. You have such a big responsibility. However, that large task is more reason to make sure that your outside is also a good reflection of the inside. Healthy. The energy and vitality that is given with proper exercise and diet is the fuel to help you act upon the goals in your life. If you have no fuel, you have no or very little movement. Also, that little guilt that is felt inside affects you and your loved ones much more than you think."

"What do you mean?" Richard wanted to make sure he was fully understanding what Mr. Smith was saying.

"Okay. Your kids want to play catch with Dad. You're too tired to play. You'd rather sit on the couch, grab the remote, and check out. Your mind is saying you should, but your body is saying no. It's too tired. You just don't have the energy. Your wife tells you she is taking that class at the gym. She's excited. However, you immediately make her feel guilty by responding with, 'Wow, I wish I had time to work out. Must be nice.'"

"That's makes sense."

"Those are just the little things. How about the possibility of leaving your family earlier than you wanted?"

"You mean dying?" Richard asked in a serious, humbled tone.

"Yes. We never know when our last day will be on this Earth, but we should attempt to not race to that day. We need to take care of our body. It is the only one we have while on this Earth. Feed it, and exercise it properly. As we have said, when you take care of yourself, you can than be a blessing to others. If you have no energy, lying in a hospital bed, or, worse, lying in a grave, how can you then reach your great destinations, much less have the incredible joy of watching your loved ones reach theirs?"

Mr. Smith stopping the walk and faced Richard, as he did on previous walks, to make sure his point was getting across. He then placed both hands on Richard's shoulders. "You have to make your health a priority. Too many good, motivated people leave this fact out of their lives. The result is a shortened life that still had so much that could have been given. So many talented individuals don't do well because they simply do not feel well. You have an incredible amount that you can give, Richard. I can see it in you. It will be hard to use your talents and gifts if you do not have the vitality to do so."

"You are so correct. You are not saying I should become a fitness junkie, but I should take care of the body that God has given me. Then I will have the energy to go after my goals, give back to the ones I love, and be an example for future generations. Make it not a should, but a must." Richard made sure he knew and wanted to reassure to Mr. Smith that he understood.

"Got it! You said it perfectly. I knew you would be good at this. You have an incredible future ahead of you, young man."

Richard heard the words of Mr. Smith and the certainty in them and felt a chill come over his body.

Incredible future? Good at this? What is Mr. Smith referring to?

They approached Richard's driveway and said their usual good-byes. Halfway up his driveway, Richard stopped and turned around. He watched Mr. Smith continue down the leaf-cluttered road. As Mr. Smith walked, Richard, through the moonlit night, noticed the leaves began to collect and swirl around the old man's legs. It was as if a small wind tunnel were forming around him. Mr. Smith continued, almost unaware of the activity that was surrounding him. At that point, he seemed to fade into the night and almost disappear. Richard squinted and tried to find Mr. Smith, but he was gone.

Must be too dark. Either way, it was another great lesson learned.

CHAPTER 7
TENACITY GOT THE WORM

A nother week went by. Richard implemented what he was being taught. He was taking action.

***

"Richard, have you ever ordered a book and never finished it?"

"I do struggle with that. It sometimes depends on the book, but I think my real problem is just taking the time to finish it."

"What about starting to exercise and then stopping after a few weeks?"

"Yes, that as well. At least I'm not the only one. It seems like a constant struggle for everyone."

"It is. You're right. What about a goal or something you thought you really wanted to achieve, but, once you started, you stopped because it became a little harder than you thought."

Richard started to become aware of where this next lesson was going. "You mean quit?"

"Yes. That's what I mean."

"I have, but everyone has."

"Do you want to be like everyone?"

"If you put it that way, no, I do not."

"Richard, what I have found over my life is that there really is no easy way to live your dreams. Plain and simple, it takes hard work. Now, most people start working hard on their dreams. But most people cannot work hard on their dreams for too long. Most people do not see it through."

"So you are saying you have to tough it out and stay in the game?"

"Yes, you can say it that way. So much of success is just hanging around and staying the course when others have decided to abandon ship. Too many people start to feel the pressure and weight of the work needed to accomplish their goals and then say no more. What they need to understand is the pressure and weight molds us so we are able to handle the goal when it is accomplished. Can you think of something in nature that is under enormous pressure?"

Mr. Smith paused while Richard tried to think of an answer.

"A diamond is under pressure," Richard answered excitedly. He was able to actually come up with an answer.

"Perfect! A diamond. A piece of coal becomes one of the most precious and sought-after gems because it simply hangs in there and it's under incredible pressure. Yes, I know it doesn't have a choice. The problem for us is that we do. When we often feel the pressure, we exercise the wrong choice, and we give up. If we want to become precious, rare, and sought-after, we have to stick in there like that diamond. We must let the pressures, obstacles, and hardships shape us."

"That makes perfect sense. We give up too soon on our dreams. Heck, we seem to give up too soon on most everything, like marriage, kids, jobs, and fitness."

"Well, yes. That's why true success is rare. That's why diamonds are rare. Very few hang on and see it through. When others have given up and moved on, the person who stays and fights when the going gets tough will be the successor."

"You have made me realize that I have given up too soon on dreams I had in the past. You've made me realize that, if we do want to become better, to become precious and rare, we must endure the enormous pressure and let it mold us in becoming the individuals we want to become. What were some of your biggest obstacles?" Richard asked Mr. Smith.

Mr. Smith stopped walking, but he did not turn to face Richard this time. With Richard's eyes adjusted to the night, he could see Mr. Smith slowly shut his eyes. At that point, Richard felt a warm breeze almost engulf his body. The night was otherwise cool, so Richard found it odd. *Colorado weather.*

"Richard, I have endured much in my life as a young boy and as a young man, including the separation of parents, the loss of one, and the confusion of searching for things in wrong places. I started a relationship and then a family, not knowing what my role should truly be. It is life. Life is hard. Life is pressure. Life is pain. However, as mentioned, I was able to meet someone in my life who showed me how life could be so much more. He taught me very much like I am teaching you, and it made all the difference."

"What was his name?" Richard asked.

Mr. Smith opened his eyes and began to walk again. For only the second time since they met, he felt uncomfortable. He had the same feeling come over him as he did while standing outside Mr. Smith's home that afternoon. It was like he wasn't supposed to be there, like he wasn't supposed to ask that question.

"He was a grand ol' man. Name does not matter as much as the lessons he spoke into me and now I am passing to you," Mr. Smith answered.

Richard didn't want to pry. They finished the last minutes of their walk and talked about Richard's family. On every walk, Mr. Smith seemed to always want to be caught up on the activities in Richard's life. Richard enjoyed telling the funny little things his children would do. Mr. Smith seemed to soak it all in, as if they were his children. Mr. Smith always remembered the little incidents Richard told him. Sometimes, Mr. Smith would remember the stuff that Richard forgot. Richard loved the fact that Mr. Smith truly seemed to take an interest and care about his family when Mr. Smith had actually never met them.

CHAPTER 8
ATTITUDE GIVES ALTITUDE

It was a cold night. Along with the wind, there was a light rain falling that plastered the leaves to the road. Richard enjoyed the rain. They didn't get much, so, when they did, it was refreshing. He loved the smell the rain gave as it seemed to wash all that it touched. It was as if all around was getting cleaned and smelled better because of it. The smell of dust was disappearing. A new freshness was in the air.

It seemed a little darker than the usual Friday night walks. Maybe it was the sliver moon giving little help that evening. Whatever it was, it made it harder for Richard to see his usual distance ahead.

Hopefully, Mr. Smith will be able to see me coming.

On all their walks, Mr. Smith always seemed to appear at the same place as Richard approached his home. Richard assumed Mr. Smith was just able to see him coming. It was too dark tonight. Richard couldn't see fifteen feet in front of him. He continued ahead and enjoyed the sound of the rain falling as it soothed his mind. Richard's weeks were getting better. He was making progress, and it all had to do with his relationship with Mr. Smith.

He got closer to Mr. Smith's home. The large silhouette leaning up against the mailbox startled Richard. Richard, not being able to see in front of him any great distance, was unable to notice his friend until he was about ten feet away.

"You startled me. I didn't see you there." Richard sighed as if to release the surprise he felt.

"I'm sorry about that. What a beautiful night it is. The rain is so refreshing. It also seems to give a person a little more boost sometimes."

"Maybe we should ask the people in Seattle and see what they think," Richard joked.

"True. If it rained most of the time, we might not enjoy it as much when it did. Absence makes the heart grow fonder. That must be true with rain as well."

The two men walked and took in all the smells and sounds of the night while enjoying one another's company. Richard felt an incredible sense of comfort and security. It was a safe feeling that he only experienced when he was around Mr. Smith. Sure, he enjoyed other people, but this was different. It was really hard to explain the feeling. He had tried to explain to Renée, but, not wanting to make her feel inadequate, he didn't fully disclose the overwhelming feeling he experienced with his new friendship. It was special and life-changing.

"Richard, two brothers grew up with a rough childhood. Their father was an alcoholic, which made their childhood challenging, to say the least. One brother spent most of his life in and out of prison. He eventually ended up homeless. The other brother became incredibly successful, both in the workplace and home. The two brothers were asked why they became who they were. The homeless brother responded, 'My father was an alcoholic.' The other brother was asked that same question. He said, 'My father was an alcoholic.' You see, Richard, the two completely different attitudes they chose about the same situation gave such different results."

Richard soaked in the lesson and nodded his head. "What a difference. One chose to learn; the other chose to blame."

"Correct. Our attitude shapes so much of our lives. The attitude we have shapes the choices we make in our lives. If our attitude is poor, then our choices will be poor."

"I can see that. I know that, when my attitude is bad, there seems to always be a string of stupid decisions that follow."

"As we mentioned before, life can be and is hard. We don't need a bad attitude to make it any harder. That doesn't make sense. The last time I checked, I haven't heard of too many pessimistic people changing the world."

Richard laughed. "That is so true."

"Good attitude gives energy to each day; bad attitude just drains. Having the correct attitude will not only help you, but help those around you. You can become a person of attraction, not distraction. You can become someone who gives energy, not someone who takes it away. People want and are attracted to people they like, people who give them energy and hope, people who admire and encourage them, people who inspire and see in them what they might not see in themselves. That is the kind of person others want to be around."

"You're so right. I know of a few people in my life that, when I'm done visiting with them, I feel as if my tank was filled with fuel and I'm ready to conquer the world. There are others, however, that, when we're done, I want to go to sleep and try to forget the conversation ever took place."

"Our attitude shapes so much of who we are. If you have an incredible attitude in life, you will more than likely have an incredible life. Now, I'm not saying hardships will not come. We all know they will. With a correct attitude, however, you will be able to make proper decisions that will bring you out of that hardship much faster."

"You can also say that, if you have a poor attitude, you will have a poor life."

"That is true. You may acquire money, but I have seen many wealthy men who are the most unfulfilled and negative people I know. They have money in the bank, but that's about it. As we know, that is not success."

They continued their walk and enjoyed the rain that continued to fall. Mr. Smith had on his usual fedora; Richard wore a baseball cap. Occasionally, the wind would steer the rain a little sideways and dampen the face of the two men. It was a cold night, so it gave the sensation of small pricks to the face.

Their walk ended. Richard knew he needed to be more aware of his attitude. Just being aware seemed to be half the battle.

Isn't it for us all?

CHAPTER 9

GET OUT OF THE CAVE: THE GIFTS OF RELATIONSHIPS

Richard's weeks had been steadily improving. The lessons he had been learning with Mr. Smith were beginning to make a positive impact in his life. He started each day being thankful, along with reviewing his goals. It gave Richard a tremendous sense of purpose. He knew what he was working for and toward. He was also taking time to care for the body he was given. With his exercise and better diet came energy and a great self-esteem. No longer was he living his days guilty for missing workouts or eating what he knew was not healthy. This new discipline wasn't easy, but, as Mr. Smith had told him, he needed to see it through. In order to be extraordinary, you had to do things differently than the average. The average for most was to quit and give up. Richard, however, was becoming more disciplined and appreciated the results that seemed to follow.

Richard was also very aware of his attitude. Before knowing Mr. Smith, he could get upset in an instant. It wouldn't take much to turn a day into one filled with anger, disappointment, stress, and depression. Richard began to be aware of what he was putting into his mind and made sure it was information that would lift his spirits, not bring them down.

Richard was always excited as to what his next lesson would be. He cherished his weekly time with Mr. Smith. The forty-five minutes the men were together were powerful for Richard. There was still more to learn, however. It was as if he were getting a full-service tune-up while being filled with high-octane fuel. As he approached Mr. Smith's driveway to see him standing in the same place, he always knew tonight would be no different.

After the warm greeting and catching up from the week, Mr. Smith started the next lesson. "What number are we on?"

"I'm sorry. Do you mean which number lesson?"

"Precisely."

"Number six."

The two men walked close together. Because the nights were getting colder, it seemed to help. Richard looked over at Mr. Smith, who then gave him a slight smile.

"Oh, yes. Number six. A very important one. They are all important, but, for some, this is the one many miss because they fall short of a life they could have had."

"I don't want to fall short."

"You won't. I can guarantee you that." Mr. Smith responded with confidence.

"I appreciate your assurance in me."

"You are welcome. Now onto the lesson. Let me start with a very basic question. Does a baby need to be held, touched, and spoken to?"

"Of course. It is vitally important for growth. If a baby is neglected too much, it can obviously lead to death."

"So you are saying that the interaction a baby has with another human is important for its growth. If it does not have that proper development, its life is put at risk?" Mr. Smith gave more of a statement as opposed to a question.

"Yes, the relationship is vital."

With a sense of discovery and excitement, Mr. Smith replied, "Ah, you said relationship. You are really much smarter than you give yourself credit."

"Why thank you."

"You see, Richard, we do not live in a cave. We need each other. In order for us to be successful in our marriage and with our children, coworkers, and clients, we must master the art of relationships. We need to become a person of value in other's lives."

"What do you mean?"

"Great question. Some examples may help. Do you know what your wife values in you?"

"I think I help her around the house. You know, with the dishes and putting the kids to bed. That sort of stuff."

"First of all, I'd say you need to not guess, but know 100 percent. Once you understand what others value in you, it then gives you the ability to be able to give them more of that value. Too often, we don't know what others need or value in us. We guess and often get it wrong."

Richard slowed his walk for a moment as if to sink in all that Mr. Smith had just said to him. He wanted to make sure he was understanding this important lesson. Like many men, he was often confused in the area of relationships.

"You're right. If I think about it, what I value in my wife is completely different from what she values in me. If I try to give her what I value in her, then she will not be satisfied. I need to give her the value she wants from me."

"We have heard this so many times. You have to speak her language. Well, it is true. It is also true that, behind every happy and successful man, is a woman whose needs are being met by that man."

"When Mama ain't happy, then nobody is," Richard joked to Mr. Smith.

"Richard, relationships are also incredibly crucial outside of the home, no matter if it's the waitress at a restaurant or an important client. How you relate and make that individual feel will make all the difference in the world. You have to be someone that people want to be around. People want to be around others who add value to their lives."

As they continued their slow pace and took in the refreshing night air, Mr. Smith continued, "There is one other point I need to make in regards to relationships, Richard. It is the one I mentioned earlier that prevents many people from achieving extraordinary success. It is a fact we all need to understand. If we want to achieve what seems like impossible dreams and goals in our lives, we must partner with other individuals who fill in where we are weak. We cannot think we have all the answers and know it all. If we think in that manner, we will only go as far as our abilities can take us. That is not as far as we may like. However, effective partnering can take you to destinations you would have thought you never could have reached."

"The destinations I could have never reached using just my ability." Richard wanted to clearly understand what was just said.

"Relationships and partnering will be one of the most important areas of your life. They can be some of our greatest joys and slingshots to success, or they can be some of our biggest failures in life."

"Understood. I see this so much with families and businesses being torn apart. It's scary."

"It is. Scary and risky, but necessary."

Coming to the end of their walk and approaching Richard's driveway, Mr. Smith turned to face Richard. "You need to first become that incredible person of value and integrity. A great speaker once said that, in order to attract attractive people in your life, you must first become attractive. Become that person."

"I will."

The two men said their usual good-byes as their walk ended. Mr. Smith continued up the road toward his driveway. Richard watched his mentor fade into the dark night. He was eager for their next walk.

CHAPTER 10

THE LIFELONG PLAN: NEVER STOP LEARNING

"Daddy, are you going on your walk tonight?" Richard's middle boy, Ty, asked.

"How do you know Daddy walks on Fridays?"

"From my window, I see you leaving. I wait to watch you come back."

"Well, I didn't know you did that, young man. Your little buhookie is supposed to be in bed." Richard laughed as Ty got a big smile on his face.

"Do you ever get scared, Daddy? Walking alone in the night?"

"Alone? I walk with Mr. Smith."

"Who's he?"

"He's my walking partner and a great friend of your dad."

"I've never seen you walking with anybody, Daddy. I always see you walking alone."

Richard was a little curious as to why Ty did not see Mr. Smith. Renée came into the room.

"What are you two talking about? Our little boy needs to get to bed. You need to take your walk. You won't want to keep Mr. Smith waiting."

"You're right. Our little man needs to get to bed, and Daddy needs to get walking."

"Okay, Daddy. Have fun on your walk."

Richard and Renée tucked Ty tightly into his bed and then proceeded to make sure the other three were all secure in their rooms for the night.

Richard stepped out into the chilled night. As he walked out to the road, he glanced back to see Ty's outline peeking through the upstairs bedroom window.

Just as he said. Watching his daddy.

Richard just let Ty watch. He did not make any reference that he could see his boy. Richard turned back to the pavement and continued up the road. Richard could see clearly, as the moon lit up the night. It was very opposite from the last two Friday walks in which he couldn't see Mr. Smith until he was right next to him.

Richard greeted Mr. Smith much differently than he did eight weeks ago. He was more relaxed and more genuine. "My friend, wonderful to see you this energizing night."

"Wonderful. What a nice greeting you give me. I can tell you feel good tonight."

"I do feel good. I owe much of it to you."

"Ah, you, however, have been doing the work. You have become more disciplined."

"You were right. We need to learn to love discipline, and I have. Thank you." Richard placed his free arm and left it on the shoulders of Mr. Smith as they continued down the familiar road.

"Richard, you mentioned we need to learn to love discipline. Besides discipline, what do you think is the other important word in that statement?"

Richard thought for a moment. "Love?"

"That is a good guess, but not correct."

Richard whispered the statement to make sure he did not answer wrong again. "Learn. Is it to learn?"

"Correct. We need to never stop learning. As obvious as this statement may sound, it is not apparent in the majority of people's lives. For many, the last book they read from cover to cover was required reading in a senior class in high school or college."

Richard missed Mr. Smith's first question and suddenly did not remember the last book he read. He was not as enthused as he was at the beginning of their walk. Sometimes, he did feel very much like a student who occasionally felt inadequate. Although he was experiencing less of that feeling, it still happened.

Mr. Smith sensed Richard's change of attitude. He placed his large hand on one of Richard's shoulders. "If you haven't read a book in a while, that is okay. It can only get better."

"If you look at it like that, you're right. I think the last book I may have read was the instruction manual to my car because I was bored while waiting for a client. Does Dr. Seuss count?"

"No. I am sorry. Children's books do not count."

"There really are three areas where people must continue to learn, no matter how old or young. They first must read great books. It is amazing how much inspiration, ideas, and direction can stir in one's soul when he digs deeply into books that teach. Reading inspiring autobiographies of great leaders, small parables that ignite our fires, or publications that direct and guide the way we live our lives are key to becoming better."

As the men walked, Richard's mood was beginning to lift as he listened to Mr. Smith.

"Richard, over 92 percent of people who buy books never get past the first chapter."

"I've heard that before."

"Here is this wealth of information and answers to what they may be struggling with, and they choose to not discipline themselves enough to read it. Instead, they head to the TV to not think. They just zone out as if the act of zoning is somehow going to fix their problem."

"I'm guilty of that. Sometimes, it just feels good."

"Understood. Just be careful not to get too comfortable. People often sit down. That then becomes the position for the next three to four hours. Then routine sets in. Do not get to that point. Instead of picking up the remote, pick up a book. That is the wiser choice."

This would be foreign to Richard, but he was willing to try it because all that Mr. Smith had been teaching him had been making an enormous impact in his life.

"Now to the second key area in learning. It is actually what you are doing right now."

"Learning with you?" Richard responded excitedly.

"Right again, young man. It is learning from others. Not only can we do this with great autobiographies, but we can also continually learn from others who have achieved what you are striving for. An example may be a man who has an incredible relationship with his wife. Learn from him. Invite him to lunch, and ask what he does. Sometimes, we make things much more complicated than they are. Often, we just need to have the courage to ask others how they do what they do, that is, how they have that passionate marriage, that closeness with their children, or the financial independence. Just ask."

"Sometimes, I think they won't want to share or take the time for me."

"Richard, the people who are true successes always have time for others. If you are genuine in your approach, they would love to share their story."

As Mr. Smith was talking, Richard realized how lucky he was to have this man in his life. He realized the time Mr. Smith was giving him, and it made him thankful. Richard felt lucky. He felt hope and excitement for his future.

As they came around the corner and approached the end of their walk, Richard purposely looked at his son's window to see if he could spot Ty peeking out. He noticed the outline. Richard never thought to look before Ty told him he watched him. Richard did not say anything to Mr. Smith, not wanting to distract from the lesson.

"All right. I am ready."

"Learn from yourself. Learn from your failures and your triumphs. Review your days. Make sure not to repeat mistakes made. Repeat choices and actions that lead you closer to your goals. Do not be like most who never ask themselves the question, 'Am I becoming the best person I can become?' Be better than that. Make sure to not get too comfortable. Being comfortable can be your worst enemy. Always learn, and read. Learn from others and yourself. Just never stop learning."

Mr. Smith gave Richard a big hug. He then turned to continue down the road.

"Thank you," Richard said softly to Mr. Smith.

Mr. Smith, already ten feet or so down the road, glanced back. "You're welcome, Richard. Now tell your boy Ty that he need not stay up so late watching out for his dad."

Mr. Smith briefly looked up to the window where Ty was watching. He turned and strolled into the night.

As Richard watched his mentor walk away, thoughts raced through his mind.

Mysterious.

CHAPTER 11

GIVE BACK: WE ARE THE HANDS

T he sun beamed through Richard's sunroof. He drove home in the early afternoon. He had a light day and just needed to go to the office to check on a few files and make an appearance. Richard was fortunate to be able to work from home when he wasn't meeting with clients at various places. So he usually stopped by the office occasionally in the week to justify the desk he was keeping. It was usually a very short visit.

As he pulled onto the road leading into his community, he had to pull over to the side to take an important call from one of his better clients. He knew notes would need to be taken. Although he was close to home, pulling over was the smartest and safest choice.

During the conversation and note-taking, Richard's eyes were drawn to Mr. Smith's home. As he attempted to listen to his client, his mind seemed to wander toward the careful studying of a home where he had never seen anyone during the day. There was no sign of the man he had grown so close to. Although Richard had never seen Mr. Smith or anyone for that matter in the day, the yard looked as though it should be featured in *Better Homes and Gardens*.

Too strange. I'll have to ask Mr. Smith how he does it. I will ask this Friday.

***

About ten minutes into their walk, Richard asked, "How do you keep your yard so immaculate? I never see you or Mrs. Smith in the yard. I actually have never seen anyone in the yard."

"I'm out there. You must not be looking hard enough."

"I'm usually pretty observant, and I can't remember seeing you at all. Otherwise, I would have stopped by or honked."

"As I said, you just need to look a little harder. I'm out there. You don't think the yard looks that way naturally, do you?"

"Well, I guess not. I will look harder."

How could I have missed Mr. Smith? I'll look harder.

"How about we get to our lesson? Heck, I'm an old man. You never know how long this old geezer will be around," Mr. Smith said jokingly.

"You look pretty healthy to me. I'm sure you have a few more years in you."

"You never know how much time you have left on this Earth. With that, each day is truly a gift. With that gift is another day you can give to others."

"What do you mean specifically by giving to others?"

"Too many people do not understand the joy of giving. Do you know what the best part of receiving is?"

"What?"

"It is then being able to give away part of what you have received. It is your opportunity to affect another person with what you have been fortunate in your life to have and make their life better. There are very few better joys in life than being able to bring greater joys to others."

As they walked, Richard listened and felt inspired inside. He was feeling excited to become a person who'd be able to give to others. He was thinking not so much about himself, but his focus was beginning to be about others and what he could do and contribute to them.

"You see, Richard, we have a responsibility. It is said that, to whom much is given, much is required. If you have been blessed in your life, you then need to bless others. As we talked about before, life is so much about relationships. Too many people have their minds just focused on themselves, like what they can get or what someone can give them. It's the what-are-you-going-to-do-for-me mentality. What they are really doing is looking for outside people or stuff to fill their desires or their happiness. As I am sure you know by now, that doesn't work. You will be disappointed. However, the people who are truly successful put others first."

It was as if a light suddenly turned on in Richard's head. He was learning so much with Mr. Smith, but this lesson seemed to place all the previous lessons in a different light, a different angle.

It isn't about me, but others.

Mr. Smith continued, "Your success is largely determined by how much you put other people first and the more people you influence in a positive way. I once heard a great speaker tell a story about what his father told him when he was a young man. His father said, 'Son, when you were born, the world rejoiced while you cried. Live your life so that, when you die, you rejoice while the world cries.'"

"I have never really thought of it that way. Society tells us so much that we need to look out for number one and no one else. To try to get as much out of someone as you can while you can."

"That is backwards. If you want to be remembered in a way that leaves an incredible legacy, you must be an incredible giver. You must be a giver of your time, resources, knowledge, and abilities. You must be a giver of yourself. That is when you become a person of value in other's lives. And that value can and will continue long after you have left this Earth."

"Thank you, Mr. Smith. I cannot tell you enough how incredibly valuable you are in my life. Our lesson tonight seemed to really open my eyes much more than they have been. Thank you so much. I'm excited for my future, but, most importantly, the future of the people I may touch."

"There you go. The future of the people you will touch. That is exciting."

The two men enjoyed the rest of their walk, discussing family and telling great stories of past trips and adventures. It was amazing the places and stories that Mr. Smith told. It was an exciting life that Richard hoped to live one day.

CHAPTER 12
THE FINAL WALK

The week went by quickly. Richard lived the week and saw the world through different eyes. No longer did he see his clients as objects to help him reach his goals, but they were opportunities for him to be able to give of himself. He focused more on truly teaching valuable life lessons to his children, as opposed to just disciplining them. Richard was beginning to think about how he wanted to be remembered not by how much he gained, but by how much he gave. All the people around him appreciated the transformation.

As Richard moved onto the pavement from his driveway, he closed his eyes and took in the crisp night air. He listened and smelled his surroundings. A certain peace always came to him before his meetings with Mr. Smith. It was a relaxed excitement.

As Richard approached, he could see the familiar position of Mr. Smith coming to meet him.

"Good evening, my friend." Mr. Smith was the first to engage.

"Good evening to you. How are you this beautiful night?"

"I'm super. I'm also looking forward to our time tonight. No lesson tonight. I want to hear about you and how things have been going in your life." Mr. Smith wrapped his big arm around Richard's shoulders.

"You mean there are no more lessons?"

"There is one more big lesson, but that is not for tonight."

Richard thought about Mr. Smith's comment. "So there is only one more lesson. What will we be studying after that one?"

"After that one, I will be going away for a little while. I have to take an important trip."

"How long will you be gone?"

"I'm not sure. It may, however, be for some time."

Richard felt a sinking feeling as he listened to Mr. Smith. He had grown so close to him. Although they only saw each other on Friday nights, just knowing that Mr. Smith lived a few houses down and their Friday time was set gave Richard a feeling of comfort. To not have Mr. Smith in his life for an unknown amount of time did not feel good.

"Is Mrs. Smith going with you?"

"No, she's going to stay. Someone has to keep up with the house and the yard, you know," Mr. Smith said jokingly as to try to lighten up the somber mood that Richard was feeling.

"May I ask where you are going and why?"

"That you will find out, but just not tonight. So, with our limited time together, let me hear about you and what has been happening in your life. Tell me, Richard. Tell me everything."

Understanding the shortness of their time together, Richard began to open up to Mr. Smith about all the positive changes in his life. He talked about his relationship with his wife, his children, and his clients. He told Mr. Smith about how he was excited to get up each morning and learn from the days. He said how he was excited for what opportunities were presenting themselves. Richard told of his dreams and aspirations that were ignited deep inside that had lain dormant for so long until he started meeting with Mr. Smith. He told Mr. Smith of the little details of playing with his children, wrestling on the floor, or jumping on the trampoline. He talked about the wonderful nights with his wife, laughing about past times, and getting excited about future experiences to come. He let Mr. Smith into all that he was feeling. As they walked, the two men both cried, laughed, and enjoyed their special night.

Approaching Richard's driveway, their time together was ending. Richard again felt the sinking in his heart. He was having to say good-bye to someone and not know how long the good-bye would be. It was hard.

"Would you at least like to come into the house for a little?" Richard asked.

Oddly, this was the first time that Richard asked the question to Mr. Smith.

"I appreciate the offer, but I wouldn't want to keep the missus waiting."

"I understand." Richard didn't want to push.

"Richard, you're an incredible man with an even more incredible future. Live up to your full potential, not so much for yourself, but for others. I know you will. I can see it. It will happen."

"Thank you."

Mr. Smith gave Richard a big hug and turned. He started to walk away.

"Will it be long until I see you again?" Richard asked.

"It will be shorter than you think."

Mr. Smith continued up the road. Richard watched and wondered when he would see Mr. Smith again. Suddenly, Richard was startled as he heard footsteps coming from his driveway. He turned and saw Renée coming.

"Honey, I want you to meet Mr. Smith. Hurry." Richard knew Mr. Smith was soon going to be out of sight.

Richard glanced back down the road and could still see Mr. Smith about twenty-five to thirty yards ahead. It was dark, but Richard could still see him.

"Mr. Smith, wait!" Richard wanted to get Mr. Smith's attention so he could at least meet Renée.

The walks had always been just the two of them. Because Mr. Smith was nowhere to be found in the day, the two had never met. Renée obviously knew about Mr. Smith and the changes she was appreciating in her husband, but they had just never met.

Renée looked up the road. "Honey, I don't see anyone."

"Renée, he's right there. You don't see him" Richard was confused as he watched his friend walk away.

"No, I don't see anyone."

Richard clearly saw Mr. Smith. "Honey, seriously, he's right there." Richard then turned back to look at Mr. Smith, but he was gone. He squinted hard and tried to see his friend one last time. All he saw was the dark, empty road.

"Richard, I don't see him."

"He's already gone."

Richard found himself having trouble sleeping that night as thoughts raced through his mind.

Where is Mr. Smith going? Why couldn't Renée see him? When will he return? Will he ever return? How does Mr. Smith seem to know so much about me? Why have I never seen him in the day? Should I stop by his home tomorrow and wish him farewell on his journey?

With his thoughts stirring, Richard decided he would stop by Mr. Smith's home in the morning to say good-bye one last time. Why this made him so nervous felt strange.

What is the big deal? It may be bigger than I think.

CHAPTER 13

MEETING MRS. SMITH

I t was a rainy Saturday morning. The family was still sleeping as Richard started brewing his morning coffee. He glanced out the window. The daylight was beginning to appear as he could see the strong winds blowing the rain sideways. He could faintly hear the whistling of the wind. The home was quiet with everyone still sleeping, which was rare with his large family. That was why Richard liked to get up early. It gave him peace.

As Richard sat in his office reading and sipping his coffee, it wasn't long before his thoughts wondered back to Mr. Smith. He had decided to stop by and say his final farewell in hopes that Mr. Smith would still be there. He didn't want to stop by too early so Richard planned to wait a few more hours. He glanced up at the large clock, as it only read six fifteen. A mix of emotions filled him. He was nervous and very anxious while also being excited to see Mr. Smith one last time before he left. He hoped he wasn't too late.

Their meetings had always been at night, same time and same place. The only changes were the weather and the lessons. Those meetings filled Richard with a powerful feeling every week. They seemed to be the fuel that kept Richard running correctly through the week. It was as if Mr. Smith were his coach and Richard would get his game plan. Then he headed back out onto the field of life. Not having him around anymore or for some time scared Richard. He had seen a tremendous change in his life for the better since their meetings. He had never been so close to his wife and children. He was creating incredible memories with them. Richard's work was flourishing. He was drawing good clients by developing the disciplines needed for his success and attractive attitude, which people wanted to be around. He was becoming an incredible giver. Richard's attitude changed to what he could give to the world, as opposed to what he could take. With that change, he became the person that others wanted to be around. It became contagious.

Would I be able to maintain this without Mr. Smith? Without my coach? Without my biggest cheerleader? Without my most trusted friend?

Richard looked out his office window and watched the rain fade as the winds calmed. He glanced high in the sky. He could see the sun just on the other side of a large storm cloud. The sun seeming to almost be pushing the cloud to the side. In Colorado, the weather was known to be able to change incredibly fast. This was going to be one of those times, as the sun was successful in its push. It made what was a gloomy, dark morning suddenly very bright. He watched as the ground began to wake up and give off a light mist as it warmed. He could see the birds and their excitement for the new day as they were warming their wings on the ground and the branches, happy for the change in weather. Richard was as well.

Almost in a daze of thought, Richard all of the sudden heard footsteps coming toward him. Their hardwood floors always seemed to give the occasional creaks in the morning as if they also needed to get ready for the high amount of traffic they would have with Richard's large family. It was still somewhat early. He wondered which child it was. He liked to let Renée sleep in. She liked it as well, so Richard was surprised when it was her.

"Good morning," Renée said sweetly. She came in Richard's office.

"Good morning to you. You're up early. What's the deal?"

"Surprisingly, I couldn't sleep so I decided to see what you were doing."

"What's racing through your mind?"

"Mr. Smith."

"What about Mr. Smith?"

"When you were done with your walk last night, I came out to see you. You called out for me to meet him, but nobody was there. You saw him so clearly, but I didn't see anyone. I didn't understand."

Richard listened to Renée. He was confused a little himself. He didn't really have an explanation for what happened. He saw Mr. Smith plain as day, but Renée couldn't see anyone.

"I know. I don't understand as well. There's a mystery to him. That's why I'm going to his house in a little bit to wish him a safe trip and thank him again."

"Safe trip? He's leaving?" Richard hadn't told Renée that last night might have been his last walk with his friend.

"Yes. He told me he was going away, but didn't say where."

"Well, you should definitely try to wish him a safe trip and say good-bye one last time. He has meant so much to you. His lessons have changed our family for the better in such a short time. I can't believe I've never meet him. Maybe I should come with you. I'd love to meet him."

"I can't believe you have never met him as well. He always seemed, however, to know the little things about our family. It was as if he knew our mind and hearts. It was as if he were watching. Maybe you should. What time is it?" Richard was anxious. He didn't know if it were late enough to knock on his friend's door.

"Seven thirty."

"Early enough. We'll leave a note for the boys that we took a walk and will be right back. Heck, they'll just turn on the cartoons and never know we were even gone."

Renée and Richard both put on light jackets as the mornings were beginning to get colder. The sun was out, which helped. With the wind, the mornings were very crisp. Richard started to feel a mix of emotions. He felt excited, anxious, scared, and nervous. It was very similar to when he went to Mr. Smith's home in the daytime several weeks prior, only to be called away by an important phone call. It seemed as though Renée might have been feeling the same as well.

Just when they were about to head out the back door, they heard their little girl cry through the monitor. Sarah was two years old and usually woke up in a happy mood. She played with her dolls for a while before wanting out of her crib. Not this morning, however. She was upset.

"I'll just stay. If Mr. Smith isn't leaving until later, maybe we can all come by and meet him," Renée said.

"Okay. I really want you to come, but I will be quick."

Richard kissed Renée and headed out the door. He didn't know what lay ahead.

***

Stepping onto the pavement, Richard fixed his eyes ahead on the tree-lined road. As he walked, he watched as the large trees begin to sway and wake up with the alarm of the morning wind. The ground was beginning to dry quickly from the night and early morning rain. It gave a fresh, clean smell to the air. Richard could see the mailbox where the two men met every Friday night.

As he came closer to Mr. Smith's home, he was able to notice that it looked different from before. He noticed the grass was taller and not manicured like that of a fairway. He also noticed the landscaped mounds were scattered with weeds and the water features were stagnant, unlike just the previous day. Richard stepped onto the once-weedless driveway of Mr. Smith. While approaching Mr. Smith's home, he felt a wave of calm enter his body. This was a feeling very opposite that what he thought he would feel and had felt in the past. As Richard looked around and approached the front door, what he thought should have been confusion about the change in the appearance of his surroundings was not so. He noticed a grey SUV in front of the garage. He had never seen it before.

Standing in front of the door, he observed the dust that had blown in and formed in the corner of the entry. When Richard stood there before, there didn't seem to be one speck of dust on the property.

Richard rang the doorbell. Not hearing anything at first, he suddenly could hear fast-approaching footsteps. The door opened. Standing in front of him was a young, handsome man. Richard thought he was most likely in his early twenties.

"May I help you?" the young man asked politely.

"I am looking for Mr. Smith. Is he still here?"

Richard could see the young man's expression change as if the question confused him. "Sir, Mr. Smith hasn't been here for some time. He passed away eight years ago."

Taken aback, Richard didn't want to seem like a lunatic. He responded calmly, "How can that be? I'm a neighbor just down the road. I was just walking with him last night."

"I'm sorry, sir. It wasn't my grandfather you were walking with. I can assure you that."

The sound of an old woman in the background interrupted the two men. "Jace, who is at the door?"

"It is one of your neighbors, Grandma."

"Let him in, dear. I want to see him," Mrs. Smith responded.

The young man stepped closer to Richard. He wanted to say something before letting Richard in. "My grandmother became very sick last night. I'm not sure how much longer she will live. I was the first relative here. I don't live too far away. My father, uncles, and aunt will be here shortly. She keeps saying it is her time to go be with my grandfather. I'm just saying this to you so you are aware."

"Thank you. I won't be long. I appreciate you letting me in." Richard was incredibly calm, but, at the same time, his mind raced inside with confusion.

Stepping into the house, the young man led Richard down a long hallway. Wanting to keep pace, Richard was unable to clearly focus on what seemed like hundreds of pictures of family, past memories of trips taken, and wonderful family moments. At the end of the hallway was a large family room with just as many pictures. Richard's eyes quickly focused, however, toward Mrs. Smith, who was sitting in an old leather chair next to a large fireplace that was adding heat to the room. He noticed a matching chair on the other side that he assumed was Mr. Smith's.

"Sit down, please," Mrs. Smith said quietly.

"Thank you." Richard headed toward a smaller wooden chair up against the wall.

"No. Not that chair. The one next to me, please." Mrs. Smith motioned toward the large leather chair that was positioned just a couple feet away from her, the one he thought must have been Mr. Smith's.

Not wanting to say no, Richard obliged. As he sat down, he looked closely at Mrs. Smith. She did the same toward him. Richard could tell she must have been a beautiful woman when she was younger. Although she was near her last days, she still had a twinkle in her eyes. She smiled softly as Richard sat down.

Just then, Mrs. Smith's grandson's phone rang. He excused himself and stepped out the back door to take the call in private. This left Richard and Mrs. Smith alone.

"You have a lovely home, Mrs. Smith." Richard wanted to break the silence.

"I have been waiting for you," Mrs. Smith responded.

Richard was confused. "You have been waiting for me?"

"I have. You are just like I remembered. It's been eight years since I've seen your face and close to forty years since I have seen you like this." Mrs. Smith smiled with what looked like the last amount of energy she had.

Richard didn't understand what Mrs. Smith was saying at all. He was starting to believe she might be delusional.

"I'm sorry, but I don't remember meeting you eight years ago," Richard responded politely.

"Maybe this will help." Mrs. Smith reached her frail arm toward a tattered envelope that sat on a small, round table next to her chair. "Read this."

Richard leaned forward and took the envelope from Mr. Smith, all the while looking into the old woman's seemingly familiar eyes. It was dated November 21, 2002, exactly eight years from today. He opened the envelope to find a letter. He started to read:

Dear Richard (or should I say Mr. Smith),

As you read this, I am sure you are very confused. Do not worry. You are sane. This is real. You are me. The beautiful women who is now looking into your eyes with her last breaths is your wife. You see, I am you. You ask yourself, 'How can this be?' I cannot answer that question. If I did, you would not understand. When you get to where I am, you will, but, while on this Earth, there are just certain things that are too much for man to understand. I want to leave you with this letter, as I will not be coming back for our walks. It is time for me to be with our love of our life, Mrs. Smith. I want to let you know that the lessons we have learned will have an incredible impact in your life. When you practice the principles daily, it will be amazing what happens in your life. I know because I have lived it. You will go on to achieve amazing things. Your marriage will be one of the greatest blessings in your life with a love that will grow each and every day. Your children will grow to be incredibly fulfilled and successful adults and wonderful parents themselves. You will touch the lives of millions of people, Richard, while speaking all over the world and helping others live a fulfilled life. You have an exciting future ahead of you, a big responsibility I know you will handle well. Out of all the lessons we have learned, there is one I want to end with you. This will be the one that will make your incredible future all possible. Without it, this future will not happen. It is the source that will give you the ability to touch so many lives in an amazing way. It will be your guidance and your source of strength while on this Earth. This lesson is to seek God's will for you always searching for his path for your life. That is where true success will come. That is where happiness and joy will find you. It is in the relationship with your Savior. From this moment, as you read this letter, Richard, you need to understand this. The blood of Jesus saved you, and you know this. You asked for this forgiveness some time ago. From this day, however, you need to start living your life as so. Enough with just sitting in the pew on Sundays and thinking about football. Enough with not opening your Bible. Enough with never praying. Start today to walk daily with God by your side. With that decision, your life will forever change down a path you could have never imagined. I leave you now, excited for your future. It is a good one. It will take work. It will not always be easy. However, you will look back, as I did, with a tremendous sense of satisfaction and comfort knowing you lived the best life you could have with dreams realized and millions of lives changed. You know that the gift of a very important decision has an amazing eternal reward, heaven. Play your part well, Richard. I know you will.

Mr. Richard Davis

Richard looked up with tears in his eyes. He reached forward and took the small, fragile hand of Renée as he looked deep into her eyes. He could see the women he loved and continues to love.

Could this be? Impossible?

He then remembered that all things were possible with God. Some we would never understand while here on this Earth. That Richard would have to go and live the life he was meant to live.

Richard and Mrs. Smith continued to hold hands and look into each other's eyes. No words were said. It seemed as though Mrs. Smith just wanted to quietly study the man she loved and continued to love. They could faintly hear their grandson finishing his conversation. Richard knew their time together would end.

"Thank you for all you have done. I could have never become the man I did without you being such an incredible support in my life. I love you." Richard fought back the tears.

Mrs. Smith smiled. "No, thank you. You have given me an incredible life with no regrets. A women could not have asked for a better man than you. Now go and live that life. I am waiting for you at home." Mrs. Smith smiled. "I have to go now and take my eternal walk. I love you."

Richard watched as the love of his life took her last breath. He felt her hand soften in his and realized she had passed. Richard felt incredible comfort and peace knowing she was going to a better place, a place in which she would meet her heavenly father and once again be reunited with him or, should he say, Mr. Smith.

***

Richard slowly walked down the hallway as he left Mrs. Smith's home. Not truly knowing what Richard was to him, Jace did not pay too much attention as he left. He was busy calling the family and letting them know what had happened. Richard walked slower than when he came in. He felt excited for his future as his quickly glanced at hundred of photos in the hallway that made it obvious the rewarding and exciting life that lay ahead. Wanting it to be somewhat a mystery, Richard decided not to look in detail as he walked and took in quick glances. He thought it better that way.

As he opened the door out of Mrs. Smith's home, he felt chills come over his body. He thought about what just happened. It felt like a dream. It was an impossibility. Stepping out, however, and feeling the Colorado air blow slightly on his face, he knew it was no dream. Richard walked back toward his home, excited for the life he would live.

MR. SMITH'S LIFE LESSONS

B e thankful. Pursue with a thankful heart. From a thankful beginning, one can move forward. Seek your passion. Go after the dreams buried deep within your heart. At that point, when action is taken, you become a light to the world. Live a healthy life. Most people don't do well because they don't feel well. See it through. If we want to become precious, rare, and sought-after, you must not crush under pressure and give up, but see it through to the end. Attitude determines altitude. The attitude we have shapes the choices we make in our lives. Great attitude equals better choices, which leads to extraordinary life. Understand the gift of relationships. People want to be around people who add value to their lives. Be that person. Engage in lifelong learning. Do not let the days take from you. Instead, take from the day all the knowledge it offers. Give back. Your success is determined largely by how much you put other people first and the more people you influence in a positive way.

Romans 10:9–10 says:

> That if you confess with your mouth, "Jesus is Lord,"
> and believe in your heart that God raised him form the
> dead, you will be saved. For it with your heart that you

believe and are justified, and it is with your mouth that you confess and are saved.

Ask yourself this question, and be honest. "If you died right now, where would you go?"

DISCUSSION GUIDE AND WORKBOOK

Well, I do hope that you enjoyed the book and are now inspired to ask yourself some serious questions and take action. If you have gotten this far, then a congratulations is at hand (unless you just went right to the back). Close to 92 percent of adults never get past the first chapter of a book, much less finish it. I like to say that my book is better than average, but, for most, better or worse, they just don't see it through.

I once heard an audiotape in which a famous speaker said, "You don't have to be great to start, but you do have to start to be great." This is your opportunity to start. Find a quiet place, grab a pencil, clear your mind of all other distractions, and dig into the questions below. As mentioned above, you have to start. Well, now is that time.

BE THANKFUL

1. In the space below, take five minutes to list all the things you are thankful for in your life. I mean everything.

_____

_____

_____

_____

_____

2. How did that make you feel?

_____

_____

_____

_____

Start each morning by counting your blessings. It is hard to feel depressed and down when thankfulness is flowing through you daily. You have to, however, make the choice to be thankful. Choose wisely.

SEEK YOUR PASSION

1. Are you currently seeking your passion?

    Yes   No   Maybe

2. What is your passion? What would get you excited to do each day? What do you love?

    _____

    _____

    _____

3. What is holding you back from pursuing that dream?

    _____

    _____

    _____

4. Have you seriously set a clear roadmap with goals, steps, and
    actions to help you accomplish that dream?

Yes   No

If no, why not?

_____

_____

_____

_____

_____

_____

If yes, are they written down on paper? Are your reviewing and
working toward them daily with small actions that compound you to
your destination? Write them down!

_____

_____

_____

_____

LIVE A HEALTHY LIFE

1. Are you taking care of the body God has given you?

    Yes   No

2. Do you have the energy and vitality needed to go after the dreams and be the best person you can for the ones you love most?

    Yes   No

If no, write down your plan of action to begin to live a healthier life.

_____

_____

_____

_____

_____

_____

_____

_____

SEE IT THROUGH

Now that you have made some commitments, do not give up. See it through. Most people stop way too soon. They are just a few days or few months from a breakthrough they will never see if they choose to halt their progress. Remember, the small daily actions compounded over time will determine your long-term success.

1.   Are you going to give up?

Yes   No

2.   Have you had trouble seeing commitments through in the past?

Yes   No

If yes, give some examples.

_____

_____

_____

_____

_____

3. If you would have stayed committed to the above examples, what would have happened? How might your life be different from today?

_____

_____

_____

_____

_____

_____

4. Who are you going to share your commitments with that will encourage and support your journey?

_____

_____

ATTITUDE DETERMINES ALTITUDE

1. On a scale from one to ten (ten being the best), rate how good your attitude is.

    1   2   3   4   5   6   7   8   9   10

2. Are you letting others affect your attitude in a negative way?

    Yes   No

If yes, then who is that person(s)?

---

3. Is it possible to not let those people affect you so negatively?

    Yes

Notice "no" isn't listed because it is possible whether you currently think so or not.

4. Are you filling your mind with material that increases your attitude or brings it down, causing frustration?

    Yes   No

So many individuals start the day by listening, reading, or watching news that is 90 percent negative. With crime, violence, war, recession, and politics, no wonder bad attitudes set in. Be careful what you fill your mind with.

GIFTS OF RELATIONSHIPS

Name the most important people in your life. Then write what they most value in you (for example, time and acts of service).

_____

_____

_____

_____

_____

1. Are you giving the people listed above what they desire in you?

   Yes   No

2. For the ones who are not getting what they need from you, write down your plan of action to give them what they need. Be specific.

_____

_____

_____

_____

3. Do you have a mentor who is calling you up and challenging you to be the best you can be?

Yes   No

If not, write down at least one person who could greatly impact your life in a positive way if you start meeting with him on a regular basis.

Now have the courage to ask him.

LIFELONG LEARNING

1. Do you have a plan to continue to learn daily?

Yes   No

If no, in the space below, write your plan to continue your learning. (For example, I will read two books a month about parenting, or I will listen to informative audio books on my way to and from work.)

_____

_____

_____

_____

_____

It is important to turn off the TV. Instead, feed and fill your mind with good information.

2. Are you learning from the mistakes you have made?

Yes   No   Choosing to blame others

If choosing to blame others, stop it. Take responsibility for the outcomes you are receiving. Remember, Event + Response = Outcome.

Become more educated and disciplined. If you change your responses, you will start to receive better outcomes.

GIVE BACK

1. Would you consider yourself a giver?

Yes   No   Maybe

2. Would you say your thoughts are mainly focused on what others can give you, as opposed to what you can give others?

Yes   No   Not Necessarily

Besides your current form of employment, what activities are you currently involved with that you give of yourself to help others? If you don't have any, write some you will get involved in.

_____

_____

_____

_____

_____

_____

WHERE ARE YOU GOING

The following questions below are from *Share Jesus without Fear New Testament*, published in 2007 by Holman Bible Publishers.

1. Do you have any spiritual belief?

    Yes   No

2. To you, who is Jesus?

    _____

    _____

    _____

    _____

    _____

    _____

    _____

3. Do you believe there is a heaven and a hell?

    Yes   No

4. If you died right now, where would you go? If heaven, why?

_____

_____

_____

_____

_____

_____

_____

If what you believed were not true, would you want to know it?

Yes   No

If you believe you are a sinner (which we all are) and want forgiveness of your sins, believing that Jesus Christ died on the cross and rose again, you can be saved if you are willing to invite Jesus into your heart and then begin a new life walking with him. Pray these words:

> *Heavenly Father, I have sinned against you. I want forgiveness for all my sins and begin a new life with you. I believe that your son Jesus died on the cross for my sins and rose again. I give you my life. I want Jesus to come into my life and my heart so I can then start to be an incredible light for you in this world. I will then start to walk down the path you have laid for me. It is a journey I am excited to take. I ask these things in Jesus' name. Amen.*

Congratulations! Please visit **www.playyourpartwell.com** to stay connected to other Christians who are working hard to become the men and women God would want them to be. These individuals are trying to play their part well.

To book Damon for events
call(720) 231-1646
or send an e-mail to
damoneddy@comcast.net.
For more information, go to
www.playyourpartwell.com

Lightning Source UK Ltd.
Milton Keynes UK
UKOW04f1457290216

269298UK00003B/835/P